COMMON COURTESIES

1. Wait for a speaker to yield the floor before rising to ask for recognition.
2. Care should be taken not to interrupt a member who has the floor.
3. Discussion on a motion should be before the entire assembly and not whispered in small groups.
4. A chairman should avoid keeping an assembly waiting in order to complete preparations.
5. Officers on a platform and members should avoid conversation or moving about while a person is speaking or a program is in progress.
6. If it is necessary to move around while business is being carried on, avoid passing between the presiding officer and a member who has the floor.
7. Members should remain seated until the presiding officer announces the adjournment of a meeting.
8. All remarks made from the floor should be addressed to the presiding officer instead of to another member.

"COME TO ORDER!"

*Essentials of Parliamentary Practice
and Group Discussion*

BY

EMMA M. WINES

AND

MARJORY W. CARD

BOTH OF THE DEPARTMENT OF
SOCIAL STUDIES, HIGHLAND PARK
(MICHIGAN) HIGH SCHOOL

ENLARGED EDITION

THE ODYSSEY PRESS

NEW YORK

PREFACE

MANY people today find their social, religious, business and political life quite generally centered in clubs and societies. To be a good member of such a group, it is quite necessary for one to be familiar with the rules of parliamentary usage which commonly govern these organizations.

There are some excellent books to which he might turn for instruction; but a person unfamiliar with the rudiments of parliamentary law often finds them too technical and exhaustive for quick reference. Other books sometimes used by the beginner are incomplete and inaccurate.

It is the purpose of this book to serve as a simple text in parliamentary usage, complete enough for all ordinary purposes, and authoritative in correctness of form and procedure. In addition to the text, it contains models, diagrams, charts, questions, suggestions for practice, and tests.

The authorities used in preparing this text are Luther S. Cushing in *Rules of Proceeding and Debate in Deliberative Assemblies*, Rufus Waples in *A Handbook on Parliamentary Practice*, Henry M. Robert in *Rules of*

Order and *Parliamentary Practice*, and Emma A. Fox in *Parliamentary Usage*.

We are especially indebted to Mrs. Fox, who has given us much helpful advice and criticism. For a more exhaustive treatment of parliamentary law her book will be found very helpful.

August, 1929

E. M. W.
M. W. C.

PREFACE TO ENLARGED EDITION

Part I of this book was written to assist groups in conducting orderly business meetings and formal debates. The purpose of Part II is to assist leaders in guiding group discussion, and to show how the advantages of informal group discussion may be introduced into large learning groups by the use of a panel or a steering committee.

For inspiration and background we are indebted to Harry A. Overstreet in *On the Panel*, to Robert D. Leigh in *Group Leadership*, to James H. McBurney and Kenneth G. Hance in *The Principles and Methods of Discussion*, to John Dewey in *How We Think*, to S. A. Courtis, E. T. McSwain, and Nellie C. Morrison in *Teachers and Cooperation*, and to Harrison S. Elliott in *The Process of Group Thinking*.

July, 1941

CONTENTS

PART I. PARLIAMENTARY PRACTICE

Contents

PART II. GROUP DISCUSSION

PART I. PARLIAMENTARY PRACTICE

INTRODUCTION: A COMMON PREDICAMENT

THE scene is laid in any club. If you please, a Dramatic Club, and you are one of its members. But if the drama is not to your liking, we are willing to reset the stage anywhere you wish; for a dignified church meeting; for a women's club; or for an enthusiastic class meeting in any high school or college. The furnishings of the room are in keeping with your club. The essentials, of course, are a sturdy chair and a desk upon which rests the gavel of authority. These await you, if you are the honored president. Conveniently near are placed another chair, and a table with pen and ink. At this you will sit, if you are the painstaking secretary. Perhaps, if you are one of the members always ready to play an equally important part in the business of the club, you are awaiting expectantly the first tap of the gavel.

It is that time in the history of this club when interest does not lag, but everything seems to be going wrong. A motion of importance is just being put to vote.

PRESIDENT (*as assured as the Speaker of the House*): All those in favor say "Aye."[1]

---

[1] "Aye," pronounced "I," means "Yes."

"Come to Order!"

MEMBERS (*from different parts of the room*): Aye. Yea. O. K. Yes. Aye.

PRESIDENT: Contrary the same sign. (*It is evident he doesn't know how to put a negative vote.*)

MEMBERS (*in a bewildered chorus*): Aye. Aye. No. Aye. No.

(*Many, wanting to vote against the measure, say nothing and lose their votes while wondering how "Aye" can mean "No." The bewilderment increases for the President blandly leaves the result unannounced and recognizes Mr. Brown.*)

MR. BROWN (*always ready with ideas—he should have waited to explain his reasons*): I move, Mr. President, that our Dramatic Club meet fortnightly instead of once a month, so that we can put on our first play early in the season. We may have difficulty in getting the Little Theatre later and——

SEVERAL MEMBERS (*interrupting*): Support the motion.

PRESIDENT (*complacently*): You have heard the motion that the meetings——Mr. Brown, I don't quite get just your motion. Will you please repeat it?

MR. BROWN (*brusquely*): Let's have the meetings once in two weeks.

PRESIDENT (*undisturbed*): What do you think of that idea?

MISS RALSTON (*eager, and oblivious to parliamentary rules*): I move that we meet once a week.

A MEMBER (*importantly*): Second the motion.

2

Introduction: A Common Predicament

PRESIDENT (*slightly puzzled by the two motions*): Miss Ralston suggests that we meet once a week. What do you think of this idea?

(*Buzzing is heard throughout the club room. Several supporters of Mr. Brown and Miss Ralston, without regard for the chair, are exchanging opinions with those seated near. At the same time two or three more daring ones also disregard the etiquette of the occasion and voice their opinions openly. The President, who feels his assurance wavering, strikes loudly with his gavel, furnished for the purpose.*)

PRESIDENT (*unable to direct the discussion, cuts it short to restore order. Surely nothing could be worse!*): Those in favor say "Aye." (*Our doughty President will not allow this meeting to run away with him.*)

A MEMBER (*bewildered*): Mr. Chairman, in favor of once a week or once in two weeks?

PRESIDENT (*quite autocratically*): Those in favor of once a week say "Aye." (*The vote is taken as unsatisfactorily as before.*) Is there any other business?

SECRETARY (*trying to emerge from the confusion of motions*): Mr. President, the first motion was to meet fortnightly. That wasn't voted upon, was it? Shall I ignore it in the minutes?

(*The President's complacency is waning. His tendency is to substitute the noise of the gavel for rules of order. It fails him. He is left helpless, it is to be feared. . . .*)

A feeling of ignorance and helplessness has been the common lot of many who have tried to conduct or take

3

part in a meeting such as that sketched above, **without** some definite knowledge of the rules of parliamentary procedure. In the same way many a game of tennis or football has been spoiled by the ignorance of some of the players or by their disregard of rules. On the other hand, a meeting may be a pleasure as well as a success, just as a game may be, if the rules are understood and applied.

These rules for the conduct of a meeting have developed gradually through the past centuries. No one person wrote out a set of them and insisted upon their being obeyed, but as soon as men met to talk over their affairs, certain customs were used. These customs, changed to meet varying conditions, became accepted rules, which we know as parliamentary law.

There are four principles upon which parliamentary rules are built. They are:

Justice and courtesy to all
One thing at a time
The rule of the majority
The rights of the minority

By thoughtfully studying these rules and applying them, you will see the possibilities of having a swiftly moving and successful business meeting, a pleasure to both officers and members.

CHAPTER I

MOTIONS

WHEN there is any business to be presented at a meeting, a person proposes it in the form of a motion. In order to do this he must rise and address the chair by the proper title (Mr. Chairman, Mr. President, Madam Chairman, or Madam President) and wait for recognition. The chairman then recognizes him by speaking his name. This procedure is called obtaining the floor. If more than one should rise at the same time, the chairman ought to recognize the one who addresses him first.

A motion should always be introduced with the words, "I move that" or "I move to," and should contain only one item of business, clearly stated—for example, "I move that a committee be appointed to buy books and magazines for the library."

Before an assembly considers a motion, it must be seconded to show that more than one person is interested in the proposition. This may be done by obtaining the floor and saying, "I second the motion." If it is not seconded, a motion is dropped.

The chairman then states the motion, quoting the words exactly, and conducts the discussion, allowing only one member the floor at a time. In discussing a

5

motion, a person should stand while speaking, except in small meetings. He must talk only on the question under discussion, addressing his remarks to the chairman.

The motion is next put to a vote by the chairman. This is usually done by the *viva voce*[1] (by the living voice) method. By this method all those in favor of a motion vote by saying "Aye," and all those opposed vote by saying "No." The chairman must take both the affirmative and the negative votes and announce the result.

The accepted form of making and disposing of a motion is as follows:

MR. BROWN (*rising*): Mr. Chairman. (*Gives his own name if chairman does not know him.*)

CHAIRMAN: Mr. Brown.

MR. BROWN: I move that —, *or* I move to —.

MR. OWEN (*rising*): Mr. Chairman.

MR. CHAIRMAN: Mr. Owen.

MR. OWEN: I second the motion.

CHAIRMAN: It is moved and seconded that —. Is there any discussion? (*Discussion may follow.*)

CHAIRMAN: All those in favor of the motion say "Aye."

All those opposed to the motion say "No."

The motion is carried (or lost).

Whenever a motion is long or of special importance, it should be put in writing. The written motion is called a resolution and should be written in the following form:

[1]Pronounced vī′vȧ vō′sē.

6

Resolved, That the club spend one meeting a month in the study of parliamentary law.

Also, if a club wishes to express its opinion upon any subject, it does this in the form of a resolution, as:

Resolved, That it is the opinion of this club that all business meetings should be conducted according to parliamentary law.

If it seems desirable to give the reasons for offering a resolution, these reasons should precede the resolution. They are called a preamble. Each reason should be put in a separate paragraph beginning with the word "whereas" and the last one should close with the words "therefore be it." The form is:

WHEREAS, Parliamentary practice is necessary for a well-conducted business meeting, and
WHEREAS, People generally are not familiar with its rules and their use; therefore be it
Resolved, That a course in parliamentary law become a part of the course of study in all high schools.

When a resolution is to be offered, the same form for making and disposing of it is used as for motions. The form is:

1. MEMBER (*obtaining the floor*): I move the adoption of the following resolution. (*Reads the resolution and hands it to the chairman.*)
2. (*Motion is seconded.*)

3. CHAIRMAN: It is moved and seconded to adopt the following resolution. (*Reads resolution.*) Is there any discussion?

4. (*Vote is taken as on any other motion.*)

QUESTIONS

1. How should a person bring up business in a meeting?
2. What is meant by "obtaining the floor"?
3. With what words should a motion be introduced?
4. What should a motion contain?
5. Why should a motion be seconded?
6. What three things should a person remember in discussing a motion?
7. What three things should a chairman do in putting a motion to vote?
8. Why should some motions be put in the form of resolutions?

SUGGESTIONS FOR PRACTICE

[It is important to have the parliamentary forms given in the text memorized and practiced until their use becomes automatic. In this way business meetings may be conducted with order, skill, and speed.]

1. Let the teacher act as chairman and the members of the class make several motions. Dispose of these according to the correct forms.
2. Have different members of the class act as chairman and continue the practice on motions.

Motions

3. Have each member write a motion in the form of a resolution.

Fill in the blanks in the following with the proper word or words:

Mr. Brown (———): Mr. Chairman.
Chairman: — ———.
Mr. Brown: I ——— ——— the club buy a piano.
Mr. Owen (*rising*): — ———.
Chairman: Mr. Owen.
Mr. Owen: I ——— — ———.
Chairman: It — ——— — ——— that the club buy a piano.   Is there any ———?
Chairman: All those in ——— of the —— say —.
All those ——— to the ——— say —.
The ——— is ———.

CHAPTER II

KINDS OF MOTIONS

WE HAVE seen in the first chapter how new business is introduced by a motion. Such motions are called *main motions* and may be introduced only when there is no other motion pending.[1] Nearly all of the motions used in business meetings are of this kind.

There are other motions used, however, which have to do with business which has already been brought up, with the order and procedure of the meeting, or with the comfort and privilege of the assembly. These may be introduced while there is a motion before the assembly if they are made in the proper place. They are of two kinds, called:

Subsidiary motions

Privileged main motions

Subsidiary motions relate to other motions under consideration, for the purpose of changing them, disposing of them, or closing debate. They are:

1. Motion to amend
2. Motion to amend the proposed amendment
3. Motion to refer the main motion to a committee

---

[1] A motion is said to be pending when it has been brought before an assembly and has not yet been voted upon.

4. Motion to postpone definitely
5. Motion to limit debate
6. Motion for the previous question
7. Motion to lay on the table
8. Motion to allow the withdrawal of a motion
9. Raising a point of order
10. Motion to provide for the manner of voting

Privileged main motions do not refer to the motion under consideration but introduce some question which ought to be settled immediately. They are:

1. Raising a question of privilege
2. Motion on question of privilege
3. Motion to adjourn
4. Motion to fix the time or place to which to adjourn

The classifications given above include all motions that would ordinarily be made in any organization. The explanation of the purpose of these motions and of how and when they may be used is given in the following chapters. Other motions are omitted since they are rarely used.

QUESTIONS

1. When is a main motion in order?
2. What is a subsidiary motion?
3. What is a privileged main motion?

CHAPTER III

AMENDMENTS

IN THIS chapter we take up the first two subsidiary motions given in the list: to amend and to amend the amendment. These are motions very often needed. One should become familiar with their purpose and know how to use them.

Sometimes a motion is made which contains a proposal that is not quite complete or which someone would like to have changed. When this condition arises another motion may be made to change a part or all of the motion already made. This second motion is called an amendment. It must be made when the chairman asks for discussion on the first motion.

The wording of the amendment must be made to fit into the original motion. There are three proper ways to amend a motion. They are:

1. To amend by inserting or adding
2. To amend by striking out
3. To amend by substituting a word, phrase, clause, or an entire proposition

So the motion, "I move that a committee be appointed to buy books and magazines for the library," may be amended in any of the following ways:

Amendments

1. "I move to amend by inserting 'of three' after committee," *or*
2. "I move to amend by striking out 'and magazines,'" *or*
3. "I move to amend by substituting 'pictures' for 'magazines,'" *or*, "I move to amend by substituting the proposition 'that a committee be appointed to spend $100 for the library.'"

(Notice how the wording of the amendment fits into the original motion.)

An amendment must be seconded in order to be voted upon. It may be discussed.

If any of the above amendments is carried, the chairman says, "The motion to amend is carried, and the question is now on the motion:

1. "That a committee of three be appointed to buy books and magazines for the library," *or*
2. "That a committee be appointed to buy books for the library," *or*
3. "That a committee be appointed to buy books and pictures for the library," *or* "That a committee be appointed to spend $100 for the library."

(Notice how the chairman states the amended motion.)

The original motion as amended is then before the assembly for further discussion. At this time more amendments may be made and disposed of before the final vote is taken.

If the vote on an amendment is lost, the motion without the proposed change is again open for discussion. Other amendments may still be offered before the final vote is taken.

While an amendment is being discussed, another amendment cannot be made before the first one is disposed of unless it is one to change the amendment under discussion. A second amendment *must* be a motion to amend the first amendment only. Amending motions must stop somewhere. The limit has been set at two amendments to the original motion pending at one time. Notice how this works out in the following diagram:

(Original motion)—"I move that the club buy a piano."

   (Amendment)—"I move to amend by inserting 'upright' before 'piano.'"

      (Amendment to amendment)—"I move to amend by substituting 'grand' for 'upright.'"

In the above illustration, after the two amendments had been made, it would be out of order:

   1. To propose another amendment to insert "small" before "grand." (Not more than two amendments relating to the original motion may be pending at one time.)

2. To propose an amendment to substitute "used" for "upright" in the first amendment. (The second amendment must be disposed of before this one may be made.)

3. To propose an amendment to substitute "rug" for "piano" in the original motion. (The two amendments must be disposed of before this amendment may be made.)

The order of voting on a motion with its amendments is to vote on the second amendment, then the first amendment, which may or may not have been changed, and finally on the original motion with the amendments which may have been adopted.

The numbers 1, 2, 3, show the order in which the motions are voted upon.

3.   Main motion
 2. | 1st amendment
  1. | 2nd amendment

Sometimes a chairman thinks it is not necessary to take a vote on the original motion if the amendments have carried. This should always be done, however, because there may still be some who wish to vote against the entire proposition.

QUESTIONS

1. What is the purpose of an amendment?
2. When is an amendment in order?

3. In what ways may a motion be amended?

4. What should be remembered about the wording of an amendment?

5. If an amendment is carried, how does a chairman state the question to be voted upon?

6. If an amendment is lost, may another amendment be proposed?

7. How many amendments may be pending at one time?

8. On which motion must the second amendment be made?

9. What is the order of voting on a motion with its amendments?

SUGGESTIONS FOR PRACTICE

1. Ask the teacher to act as chairman to show the class how to dispose of the amendments on the following motions, and how to amend the amendments.

    a. Amend the following motion by adding to it: "I move that the club visit the art museum."

    b. Amend the following motion by substituting a word, phrase, or clause for some part of it: "I move that the high school basket ball games be held only on Friday nights."

    c. Amend the following motion by striking out part of it: "I move that the club purchase new curtains and rugs for the lounge and dining-room."

2. Have different members of the class act as chairman, and have all the members practice making motions and amending them. Each motion should be properly disposed of by the chairman.

Amendments

3. After considerable practice in amending motions, have the class make motions to amend the amendments and dispose of both amendments properly.

TEST

Test your knowledge of how to make and dispose of amendments by filling in the blanks with the correct word:

CHAIRMAN: It is moved and seconded that the club pledge one hundred dollars to the Red Cross. Is there any discussion?

MR. ADAMS: I move to —— by —— fifty —— ——.

MR. STUART: I second the ——.

CHAIRMAN: It is —— and —— to —— by —— fifty for —— ——.

Is there any discussion?

All those in favor of the —— say "Aye."

Those —— say "No."

The motion is ——, and the —— is now on the —— that the club pledge —— to the Red Cross.

Is there any ——?

All those in favor of the motion say —.

Those opposed say —.

The —— is lost.

CHAPTER IV

OTHER SUBSIDIARY MOTIONS

In this chapter we shall continue the study of the subsidiary motions. After the motion to amend and the motion to amend the amendment, you will recall that there are eight other subsidiary motions:

1. Motion to refer the main motion to a committee
2. Motion to postpone definitely
3. Motion to limit debate
4. Motion for the previous question
5. Motion to lay on the table
6. Motion to allow the withdrawal of a motion
7. Raising a point of order
8. Motion to provide for the manner of voting

These motions all relate to some business already before the assembly. There may be a good reason why more time should be given for consideration of this business so that changes may be recommended; or it may be that some other time would be more favorable for discussing and voting on it; or it may be that further discussion is a waste of time, and it would be better to take the vote immediately; or it may be necessary to consider more urgent business; or it may be necessary to decide how to take the vote on a motion.

Other Subsidiary Motions

If any of these occasions arise, a member should know which of the above motions to use and how to use it.

MOTION TO COMMIT

A motion to commit, or refer to a committee, is made in order to delay a vote until a more favorable time or to give a committee an opportunity to obtain information or to make recommendations. For example, suppose that a club is discussing a motion to buy a curtain for the stage. It is quite evident that such a question should not be decided without obtaining information about costs, materials, etc. In order to delay the vote until this information can be secured, a motion to commit or refer should be made by someone. The form is, "I move to refer this motion to a committee" or, better still, "I move to refer this motion to a committee of three, appointed by the chair." This second form saves making an amendment or another motion to take care of the membership of the committee.

A motion to commit may be made after a main motion or after a motion to amend. It may not be made if any one of the other subsidiary motions in the list has been made and has not been voted upon.

An affirmative vote on a motion to refer to a committee disposes of the main motion and its amendments temporarily. The final vote is not taken until after the committee has given its report at the next or some future meeting.   If the vote on this motion is lost, the question is still open for discussion.

This motion is amendable and debatable.

QUESTIONS

1.   What are the purposes of a motion to refer to a committee?

2.   Name several occasions when a motion ought to be referred to a committee.

3.   In what form should a motion to commit be made?

4.   If the vote on a motion to commit is in the affirmative, what effect does that have on the business before the assembly?   If negative, what is the effect?

5.   Practice referring motions to a committee.

MOTION TO POSTPONE DEFINITELY

A motion to postpone definitely means to postpone the vote on a motion until some fixed time in the future. For example, suppose a motion is made in a club to contribute fifty dollars to the American Red Cross. There seems to be a difference of opinion about the amount to be contributed, and some are of the opinion it would be better to give more time for thought to the question and to take the vote at the next meeting.   The motion to be made in this case is a motion to postpone definitely.   The form is, "I move to postpone further consideration of this motion until the next regular meeting."

20

Such a motion, if carried, disposes of the main motion and any amendments made. At the time set in the motion to postpone definitely, in this case "the next regular meeting," the question comes up again under Unfinished Business. If the vote on the motion to postpone definitely is lost, the question is still open for discussion.

This motion is amendable and debatable.

QUESTIONS

1. What does a motion to postpone definitely mean?
2. What is the effect of this motion if carried?
3. If a motion to postpone definitely is carried, when does the question come up again?
4. Practice making motions and amendments, postponing further consideration on some of them until a definite time in the future.

MOTION TO LIMIT DEBATE

A motion to limit debate limits the number of times a member may speak on the same motion, the length of time he may speak, the amount of time to be used in discussion by the whole assembly, or the time at which the discussion must be closed.

Ordinarily, a member, when he has obtained the floor, may speak as long and as often as he pleases. But there is not always time for such unlimited debate; and this may be controlled by such a motion as, "I move to limit the time of each speaker on this question to two minutes" or, "I move to limit debate on this question to half an hour."

This motion is in order whenever a debatable motion is pending.

It is not debatable, but is amendable and requires a two-thirds vote.

QUESTIONS

1. What are four reasons for making a motion to limit debate?

2. Give examples to illustrate each of these reasons.

3. What vote is required to carry the motion to limit debate?

MOTION FOR PREVIOUS QUESTION

Sometimes it seems better to stop the discussion altogether on a motion. To do this, a member moves *the previous question*. The name of this motion does not give the true idea of its meaning. It simply means that the maker of the motion wishes to stop all debate and bring the question to vote immediately.

Suppose a lengthy discussion has taken place on a motion for a club to raise money for a community fund. In such a case, a member may move the previous question when further discussion seems useless.

The form of this motion is, "I move the previous question."

If carried, this does not dispose of the question. It merely means that discussion is closed, and the question of raising money for a community fund must be voted on at once. If the previous question is not carried, the discussion continues.

When there is a motion before the assembly with several motions pending, the motion for the previous question may be made on all or on just a part of the series of pending motions. If it is moved on part of a series, the previous question is said to be qualified. When it is desired to bring any one of the pending motions to vote, the previous question must be moved on all of the subsequent pending motions as well as the motion under consideration. The following illustrates the method of closing debate and voting on a part of a series of pending motions:

1. I move that the club buy six dictionaries.

2. I move to amend by substituting three for six.

3. I move to refer the question to a committee.

4. I move to postpone consideration of the question for a week.

5. I move the previous question on the motions to refer and to postpone.

In order to close debate and vote on the motion to refer the question of buying six dictionaries to a committee, the previous question must include the motion to postpone further consideration of the question for one week.

If the vote on the previous question is in the affirmative, the motion to postpone consideration for one week (No. 4) must be voted upon first. If this motion (No. 4) is lost, then the motion to refer the question to a committee (No. 3) must be voted upon next. If the vote on this motion (No. 3) is lost, the previous question is said to be exhausted, and the main motion "that the club buy six dictionaries" with its amendment "to substitute 'three' for 'six'" is then before the assembly for further discussion and disposal. In case the vote on the motion to postpone (No. 4) should be in the affirmative, the question is temporarily disposed of and the motion to refer (No. 3) would not be put to vote. Should the motion to postpone (No. 4) be lost and then the motion to refer (No. 3) be carried, the question would be disposed of by referring it to a committee.

If the vote on the previous question is lost, the discussion goes on as though it had not been made.

The previous question is in order whenever a debatable motion is under consideration. The previous question is not debatable nor amendable and, since it suppresses debate, requires a two-thirds vote.

QUESTIONS

1. What does a person wish to do when he moves the previous question?

2 If the motion for the previous question is carried, what other vote must be taken at once?

3. What is the rule about debate and the required vote on the previous question?

4. Practice closing debate and taking the final vote on several motions.

MOTION TO LAY ON THE TABLE

A motion to lay on the table is a way of setting aside consideration of a motion. Its object may be to stop further action on a motion, to give time for more urgent business, or to consider a motion under more favorable circumstances. Suppose a member of a club has made such a motion as, "I move that our club have a banquet on Lincoln's Birthday." Much time is spent in discussion until some member realizes that more important business needs to be attended to at this meeting. Under these circumstances, he may move to lay the motion on the table. Or perhaps someone is opposed to having a banquet. He may stop action by a motion to lay the motion on the table, hoping in this way to kill the idea. The form is, "I move to lay the motion on the table."

If this motion is carried, all action stops. The question cannot be taken up again unless a *motion to take it from the table* is carried. This form is, "I move to take from the table the motion that our club have a banquet on Lincoln's Birthday." This can be done at the same meeting after some intervening business, or at some future meeting when there is no other business before the assembly.

If the motion to lay on the table is not carried, the question is still open for discussion.

These motions are neither debatable nor amendable.

QUESTIONS

1. What might a member have in mind if he moved to lay a motion on the table?

2. If carried, what effect does this motion have on the question?

3. How may this same question come up for discussion again?

4. Practice making motions, amending them, and laying them on the table.

5. Practice taking some of these motions from the table and disposing of them properly.

WITHDRAWAL OF A MOTION

A request to allow the withdrawal of a motion may be made by the person who has made the motion if for any reason he has changed his mind. As this is a request instead of a motion, the form is, "I ask leave to withdraw my motion." The chairman says, "If there is no objection, the member is allowed to withdraw the motion." If anyone objects, a vote must be taken on the original motion unless a motion is made and carried to grant the request. Such a motion may be made by any member, who should say, "I move that the member be allowed to withdraw his motion."

This request or a motion to grant such a request may be made at any time before the vote is taken on a motion. It needs no second and is neither debatable nor amendable.

QUESTIONS

1. How may a person who has made a motion withdraw it?

2. What must be done if anyone objects to the withdrawal of the motion?

3. When may a request to withdraw a motion be made?

QUESTION OF ORDER

A question of order is raised when some supposed mistake in parliamentary procedure is made by the presiding officer or by some member. The rules governing such mistakes, or disorder in an assembly, are called points of order. For example, a motion may have been made for a club to procure a lecturer on some scientific subject. The chairman, thinking that a majority voted in favor of the motion, announces that the motion is carried, without taking the negative vote. In order that everyone may have an opportunity to express his opinion, this mistake in parliamentary procedure should be corrected. This may be done by a member's raising a question of order.   It must be raised when the mistake is made.

The form is:

MEMBER: Mr. Chairman, I rise to a point of order.

CHAIRMAN: Will the member please state his point of order?

MEMBER: My point of order is that the chair failed to call for the negative vote.

CHAIRMAN (*deciding the point*): The point of order is well taken, and the chair stands corrected.

If a question of order has been raised in regard to a mistake made by a member, he should take his seat immediately and wait for the decision of the chair. The chairman may ask for advice, if he chooses, or submit the point to a vote of the assembly.   If the chairman decides that a mistake has not been made, he says, "The point of order is not well taken, and the member is in order."

If any member is not satisfied with the decision, he may appeal from the decision of the chair to the higher authority, the assembly.   The member says, "I appeal from the decision of the chair."   If the appeal is seconded, the chairman says, "Shall the decision of the chair be sustained?"   This is debatable when a debatable motion is pending, and the presiding officer may state his reasons without leaving the chair.   The question is upon sustaining the chair.   If the vote is in the affirmative, the chairman says, "The decision of the

Other Subsidiary Motions

chair is sustained." If the vote is in the negative, the chairman says, "The decision of the chair is reversed."

The question of order is never amendable and is debatable only after an appeal is taken.

QUESTIONS

1. When may a question of order be raised?
2. How may a question of order be raised?
3. Who decides a point of order?
4. Give several examples showing when a question of order should be raised.
5. Have a practice lesson in using the motions we have studied. Watch for mistakes in parliamentary procedure and have them corrected by raising a question of order.

MOTION FOR MANNER OF VOTING

A motion to provide for the manner of voting may be made at any time before the vote is taken.

The different methods of voting are by:

1. Silent assent
2. *Viva voce*—by answering "Aye" or "No"
3. Division of the house—by a show of hands or a standing vote
4. Roll call
5. Ballot

Sometimes a chairman expresses the wishes of the assembly without taking a formal vote by saying, "It is so ordered," or "The minutes stand approved as

29

read. They are approved." This is called voting by
silent assent and is used frequently in disposing of committee reports, minutes, and other routine business in
order to save time.

Viva voce is the method generally used in voting on
motions, and its use has been explained in Chapter I.

If the decision of a *viva voce* vote is doubtful, any
member may call for a *division of the house.* He should
at once rise and say, "Mr. Chairman, I call for a division of the house." The chairman then says, "A
division of the house is called for. Those in favor of the
motion will rise." After the votes have been counted,
the chairman says, "You may be seated. Those opposed to the motion will rise." The negative votes are
counted. The chairman then announces that the motion is carried or lost, stating the exact number voting
on each side.

When a club wishes to keep a record of how each
member votes on a question, the members vote in re-
sponse to a *roll call.* The chairman says, "Those in
favor of the motion say 'Aye'; those opposed to the
motion say 'No.' The secretary will now call the roll."
The record of the vote then becomes a part of the minutes of the meeting.

Voting by *ballot* means writing the vote on paper.
The advantage of this method is secrecy. It is usually
used in elections or upon occasions when for some particular reason the club votes to use this method. Tell-

ers are appointed by the chairman to pass, collect, and count the ballots.

PROBLEMS

What may a member do:

1. When the discussion on a motion seems unnecessarily long to him?

2. When he thinks the motion being considered ought not to be decided without further information?

3. When he thinks the members should not decide too hastily on a question before the club?

4. When the chairman permits another motion to be considered while there is one before the club?

5. When he thinks that members are talking too often on the same question?

6. When he thinks that a record should be kept of how the members vote on a question?

7. When he changes his mind about a motion he has proposed?

8. When he wishes to bring up a question which has been laid on the table?

9. When the discussion does not concern the motion before the assembly?

10. When the result of a vote on a question is uncertain?

11. When he is opposed to a motion and wishes to kill it?

12. When he thinks it would be better not to have it known how each member votes on a certain question?

CHAPTER V

PRIVILEGED MAIN MOTIONS

A MOTION to introduce business, such as described in the first chapter, is called an ordinary main motion. Since only one subject may be considered by an assembly at one time, this main motion has to be disposed of before another subject may be brought up.

Sometimes circumstances arise in the assembly, however, that are not connected with the main motion but are so important that they ought to be settled immediately, in spite of the fact that they do not relate to the main motion. If such is the case, a motion may be offered to handle this emergency. This is called a privileged main motion because it has the privilege of interrupting the main business.

Some privileged main motions that might be made in any organization are:

1. Raising a question of privilege
2. Motion on a question of privilege
3. Motion to adjourn
4. Motion to fix the time or place to which to adjourn

There are other privileged main motions but they are less frequently used and are therefore omitted.

32

Privileged Main Motions

A question of privilege or motion of privilege deals with disturbances, unfavorable conditions in the room, or the rights or privileges of either the assembly or a member. For example, a member may wish to have some noise stopped or to make an important announcement. He may call the attention of the chair to the situation or make a motion dealing with the question.

The form is:

MEMBER (*without waiting to be recognized*): I rise to a question of privilege.

CHAIRMAN: State your question of privilege.

MEMBER: I request that the doors be closed so that we may hear the speaker.

CHAIRMAN: Your privilege is granted. Will the usher please close the door?

or

MEMBER: As a question of privilege, I move that all those who are not members be requested to retire from the room.

(*This motion is seconded, like any other.*)

CHAIRMAN: As a question of privilege, it is moved and seconded that all those who are not members be requested to retire from the room. Is there any discussion? (*Vote follows as in any motion.*)

If the chairman decides not to grant the request, he says, "The chair does not grant the privilege."

There is one time when the question of privilege may not interrupt the main business, and that is when a motion to adjourn or to fix the time and place to which to adjourn is pending.   At any other time, it may even interrupt a speaker if it requires immediate attention.

A motion on the question of privilege is debatable and may be amended.

When the business of a meeting is finished, or all the time allowed is used, a motion to adjourn is in order. The form is, "I move that the meeting be adjourned." It is neither debatable nor amendable, but must be voted upon at once.

This motion is always in order except:

1. After it has just been defeated
2. When a member has the floor
3. When a vote is being taken
4. When a motion to fix the time or place of the next meeting is pending

If there is no future meeting provided for, this should be done sometime before the meeting closes. The way to do this is to make a motion to fix the time or place to which to adjourn. The form is, "I move that when we adjourn, we adjourn to meet at (state time or place)." It is always amendable and is debatable except when it is a privileged main motion.

These two motions concerning adjournments are usually made as ordinary main motions, but they may be privileged main motions under unusual circumstances. For example, when a motion is under consideration, it might be necessary for a majority of the members to leave to catch a train. Then a member would be privileged to interrupt the main business with a motion to adjourn.

QUESTIONS

1. Mention several unusual circumstances under which it might be necessary to interrupt the business of a meeting.
2. In what two ways may such emergencies be handled?
3. When is a motion on a question of privilege out of order?
4. When may a motion to adjourn be made?
5. How are future meetings of an organization provided for?
6. When are motions concerning adjournment ordinary main motions, and when are they privileged?

TEST

1. Test your knowledge of how to raise a question of privilege by filling in the blanks with the correct word.

MEMBER (—— *waiting to be recognized*): I —— — a question of ——.

CHAIRMAN: —— your —— of privilege.

MEMBER: I —— permission to make an important announcement.

CHAIRMAN: Your —— is ——. Will the member please make his announcement?

2. Test your knowledge of how to provide for the time and place of another meeting by filling in the blanks with the correct word.

MEMBER: I —— that when we ——, we adjourn to —— at —— in ——.

CHAPTER VI

RANK OF MOTIONS

IN THE preceding chapters we have talked about the different kinds of motions, their purpose, and how to use them. There is another essential thing to know about motions, and that is *under what circumstances they may be used*.

As some motions are more important in their use than others, it has become customary to use them in a certain definite order. This order is called the *rank* or precedence of motions.

The eight motions most frequently used after an ordinary main motion has been made are listed below, arranged according to their rank. Number 1 in the list is the lowest in rank and Number 8 the highest.

1. To amend
2. To amend the amendment
3. To commit or refer
4. To postpone definitely
5. The previous question
6. To lay on the table
7. To adjourn
8. To fix time or place to which to adjourn

When any one of these motions has been made, only

a motion of higher rank, that is, one coming after it in the list, is in order. For example, if Number 6, "To lay on the table," has been made, only Number 7, "To adjourn," and Number 8, "To fix time or place to which to adjourn," may be made. It would be out of order to make a motion of lower rank, that is, any of the first five motions in the list.

So that we may see more clearly just how this rank or precedence of motions works out, let us follow what might happen to a main motion in a well-conducted business meeting. Suppose that a motion is made "that the club spend $15 to buy books and magazines for the library." While this motion is being discussed, some member preferring that all the money should be spent for books, moves "to amend by striking out 'and magazines.'" Under the discussion of this amendment, another member, thinking that it is better to find out more definitely the needs of the library, moves that the question be referred to a committee.

On account of noise from the street, those in the rear of the room are unable to hear the discussion. At this point someone rises to a question of privilege and asks that the windows be closed. The chairman grants the privilege and orders the windows closed. This privileged main motion is necessary for the comfort of the assembly and so has a right to interrupt the business before the house.

The discussion on the motion "to refer to a committee" then continues. Another member, who is not in favor of buying anything for the library, moves "to lay the motion on the table," hoping by this motion to kill the project.

It is the opinion of another member that it is better to delay further discussion and vote on this question, and so he moves "to postpone further consideration of the question until the next regular meeting." The presiding officer at once rules this motion out of order because it is of lower rank than the motion "to lay on the table."

There are at this time four motions pending: the main motion, the amendment, the motion to refer to a committee, and the motion to lay on the table. Since no other motion of higher rank has been made, it is the business of the chairman to state these motions for consideration and to put them to vote. He begins with the one of highest rank, the last one made, and works back to the main motion. Notice how it is done.

The motion "to lay on the table," being undebatable, is put to vote immediately and lost. Had it carried, all the other motions would have been disposed of temporarily.

After the chairman has given further opportunity for discussion, he puts the motion "to refer the question to a committee" to vote. This motion is lost. If it had not been, again the pending motions would have been disposed of temporarily.

"Come to Order!"

Next the amendment "to strike out 'and maga-zines'" is further considered, put to vote, and carried. Now the main motion, amended to read "That the club spend $15 to buy books for the library," is stated by the chairman. There is no further discussion, and no other motions are made by any of the members. So the chairman puts the main motion to vote, and thus the whole series of pending motions is disposed of correctly.

To sum up the main points about the rank of motions and the order they should be voted upon, remember that:

1. Only a motion of higher rank than the one being considered may be made.
2. The last motion made, being of highest rank, must be voted upon first.

QUESTIONS

1. What is meant by *rank* of motions?
2. How can you tell which motions you may use after any motion in the above list has been made?
3. In what order should a series of pending motions be voted upon?

REVIEW TEST

Which are true and which are false statements about the use of motions?

1. A motion to lay on the table is debatable.

2. A motion to adjourn may be made after a motion to commit.

3. A motion to amend may be amended.

4. The previous question requires a majority vote.

5. A motion to lay on the table may be made after a motion to postpone definitely.

6. A motion to fix the time or place to which to adjourn may be amended.

7. A motion to adjourn requires a two-thirds vote.

8. A motion to amend an amendment is not debatable.

9. A motion for the previous question may be made on a motion to adjourn.

10. A motion to adjourn is not debatable.

11. A motion to adjourn is always in order.

12. A motion to commit may be amended.

13. A motion to postpone definitely may not be discussed.

14. A motion to amend an ordinary main motion may be made after a motion to commit.

15. A motion to commit may be discussed.

16. A motion for the previous question may be amended.

17. A motion to lay on the table may not be amended.

18. A motion to fix time or place to which to adjourn may be made after a motion to adjourn is stated.

MOTIONS COMMONLY USED

(This table should be memorized. Remember that voting on this series must always be in reverse order.)

Rank		Vote	
1.	To amend	Majority	⎫
2.	To amend an amendment	Majority	⎬ *Debatable*
3.	To commit, or refer	Majority	
4.	To postpone definitely	Majority	⎭
5.	For previous question	Two-thirds	⎫
6.	To lay on the table	Majority	⎬ *Not*
7.	To adjourn	Majority	*debatable*
8.	To fix time or place to which to adjourn[1]	Majority	⎭

Amendable {5, 6, 8}

[1]The motion to fix time or place to which to adjourn is debatable if it is made as an ordinary main motion.

THINGS TO REMEMBER ABOUT MOTIONS

Of all the motions that may be used in carrying on business, we have seen that eight of these are most frequently used after an ordinary main motion has been made. It is important to know *four things about the use of these motions:*

1. When they are in order
2. Which are and which are not amendable
3. Which are and which are not debatable
4. Which require a majority vote and which a two-thirds vote

These things are shown in the table[1] on page 42. See the chart in the front of the book for quick reference on the use of other motions.

SUGGESTIONS FOR PRACTICE

1. Have the teacher act as chairman while the members of the class practice using the subsidiary motions given in the chart and disposing of them correctly.

2. Have different members of the class act as chairman and continue the practice on the use of subsidiary motions.

---

[1]It is important to have the information given in the chart drilled on until the essentials in the use of these eight motions are mastered. With these essentials all ordinary situations in a meeting may be easily and correctly handled.

CHAPTER VII

MINUTES

A RECORD of the proceedings of a meeting is called *the minutes*. The minutes should contain these essentials:

1. Name of the organization
2. Kind of meeting
3. Place
4. Date and hour
5. Name of presiding officer
6. Approximate number present
7. Motions stated and how disposed of
8. Manner of adjournment
9. Signature of secretary

This record should be brief, but it should include all the business transacted. Each motion, with the name of the maker, and each vote taken, should be carefully recorded in a separate paragraph. Discussion on a motion should not be included in minutes.

Model Minutes

HIGHLAND PARK, MICH., February 10, 1941

A regular meeting of the Parliamentary Law Club was held in the club room, 145 Glendale Avenue, February 10, 1941.

Minutes

The club was called to order by the president, **Mr.** Spencer, at eight o'clock.

There were about twenty-five members present.

The minutes of the regular meeting of January 27 were read and approved.

The report of the House Committee on securing a new club room for its meetings was read as follows:

To the Parliamentary Law Club:

Your committee, to which was referred the motion that a new club room be secured, after careful investigation recommends that the club make use of the club room of the Public Library.

Respectfully submitted,

C. F. BREED, *Chairman*

A. McLAUGHLIN

F. G. MATSON

Miss Holmes moved the adoption of the report.

Motion carried.

Mr. Brown moved that a committee of three be appointed by the chair to arrange for the Parliamentary Law Club to visit the State Legislature.

Motion carried.

The club then spent a half hour in parliamentary practice conducted by Mr. Dawes.

Miss Hilton moved the meeting be adjourned.

Motion carried.

The meeting was adjourned at nine o'clock.

J. WILCOX, *Secretary*

"Come to Order!"

[It will be helpful to learn the essentials that the minutes should contain and the order and paragraphing used in writing them.]

1. Have several people take the minutes of each parliamentary practice meeting and write them in correct form.

CHAPTER VIII

COMMITTEES

A COMMITTEE is a small group of members of a society chosen to do some special work. Committees may be appointed by the chair or voted on by the members of the society. The first member named on a committee is the chairman, often the mover of the motion that a committee be appointed. He calls the committee meetings and gives the report to the society.

There are *standing committees* and *special committees*.

Standing committees are nearly always appointed by the chair for a definite period of time, usually for the same term as the officers, to perform certain duties specified in the by-laws.

Special committees are temporary in character and are either appointed or elected to do a definite piece of work.

A committee of the whole is made up of all the members of the society acting as a committee for discussion of some subject upon which the society is not yet ready for definite action. In order to carry on this discussion a member moves that the society resolve itself into a committee of the whole for the purpose of . . . . (He here states the purpose of committee.) This motion is in order whenever a motion to commit is in order.

If the motion is carried, the presiding officer calls someone to the chair and becomes a member of the committee. No record is entered in the minutes of what takes place during the committee of the whole. This committee may make recommendations to the society. A motion "to rise and report" adjourns the committee of the whole. The regular chairman takes the chair, the meeting of the society is resumed, and the chairman of the committee of the whole reports the work of the committee.

All committee reports should be written so that a permanent record may be kept. They should contain information or recommendations and should be signed by at least a majority of the committee. The following gives the correct form:

Model Committee Report

To the Parliamentary Law Club:

Your committee appointed to investigate the cost of securing a stage curtain for the club room has given the question careful attention and submits the following report:

Rose rep
    D. L. Brown and Co. $200.00
    J. D. Fisher and Co. $225.00

Rose velour
 D. L. Brown and Co. $700.00
 J. D. Fisher and Co. $675.00
Respectfully submitted,
E. L. GIBSON
D. A. WATSON

When a committee report contains only information or statements of what the committee has done, it is disposed of by a motion either to accept and place the report on file or to enter it in the minutes. If a committee report contains recommendations, a motion is in order to accept the report and adopt the recommendations. These recommendations may be amended before being voted upon. The report of a committee of the whole is disposed of in the same manner.

QUESTIONS

1. What is the difference between standing and special committees?

2. How are committees chosen?

3. Who acts as chairman of a committee, and what are his duties?

4. Why should committee reports be written?

5. What should committee reports include?

6. How should committee reports be disposed of?

7. What is the purpose of a committee of the whole?

8. How does a society resolve itself into a committee of the whole?

9. Who acts as chairman?

10. How is the work of a committee of the whole reported and disposed of?

SUGGESTIONS FOR PRACTICE

1. Suppose you are chairman of a committee to find out and report on the cost of a new rug for a club room; prepare your report in the correct form.

2. Suppose you are chairman of a committee to secure information and make recommendations about the annual banquet of a club; write out your report.

CHAPTER IX

CONSTITUTION AND BY-LAWS

A CONSTITUTION describes the government of an organization and is its foundation law. It tells how rules are to be made and how officers are to be chosen.

The by-laws contain rules governing the action of members and details which may be changed without affecting the constitution, which should be made more difficult to amend.

The following constitution and by-laws will serve as a model and may be adapted to meet the needs of any ordinary organization.

Model Constitution

Article I.   Name

The name of this society shall be the Parliamentary Law Club.

Article II.   Object

The object of this club shall be to make its members familiar with good usage in parliamentary procedure and to give them opportunity to practice it.

Article III.   Membership

SECTION I.   Membership in this club shall be of three classes, active, associate, and honorary.

SEC. 2.   Election to membership shall be by ballot of the members of the club, and three negative votes shall exclude from membership.

SEC. 3.   Active members shall be in honor bound to study parliamentary law and to take any part they are called upon to perform.

SEC. 4.   Associate members shall be entitled to all the privileges of the club except voting and holding office but shall have no responsibility in regard to the work of the club.

SEC. 5.   Honorary membership may be conferred upon any person by unanimous vote of those present at any regular meeting.

Article IV.   Officers

SEC. 1.   The officers of this club shall be a president, a vice-president, a secretary, and a treasurer.

SEC. 2.   All officers shall be elected by ballot at the annual meeting and shall continue in office one year or until the next annual election.

SEC. 3.   A majority of all votes cast shall be necessary to constitute an election.

SEC. 4.   Vacancies in office may be filled by special election.

Article V.   Meetings

SEC. 1.   The annual meeting shall be held the third Wednesday in May of each year.

SEC. 2.   Regular meetings shall be held from the first week of October to the third week of May, inclusive.

SEC. 3.   Special meetings may be called by the president or by any three members.

Article VI.   Quorum

One third of the active membership of this club shall constitute a quorum.

Article VII.   Amendments

SEC. 1.   This constitution may be amended at any regular meeting by a two-thirds vote, the proposed amendments having been submitted in writing and read to the club at a regular meeting at least one week before being voted upon.

SEC. 2.   By-laws may be adopted, amended, or repealed at any regular meeting by a majority vote.

By-Laws

Article I.   Dues

The annual dues of all members shall be one dollar, payable at the third regular meeting.

Article II.   Duties of Officers

SEC. 1.   The duties of officers shall be such as their titles imply and the by-laws state.

SEC. 2.   The president shall appoint all standing committees.

Article III.   Committees

SEC. 1.   There shall be three standing committees, consisting of three members each: Membership, Program, and House.

SEC. 2.   The Membership committee shall present to the club names of applicants for membership.

SEC. 3.   The Program committee shall plan the course of study for the year and shall make arrangements for carrying it out.

SEC. 4.   The House Committee shall recommend a place of meeting and shall have general charge of the club room.

Article IV.   Meetings

SEC. 1.   Regular meetings shall be held the first and third Wednesdays of the month at eight o'clock in the evening.

SEC. 2.   The order of exercises shall be:
- a.   Call to order
    (Roll call)
- b.   Reading of the minutes
- c.   Communications from the president
- d.   Report of treasurer
- e.   Reports of standing committees
    - (1)   Membership
    - (2)   Program
    - (3)   House
- f.   Reports of special committees
- g.   Unfinished business
- h.   New business

54

i. Program for the day
j. Adjournment

Article V.   Plan of Work

The plan of work shall be recommended by the Program committee and voted upon by the club.

Article VI.   Parliamentary Authority

(*Title of book*) by (*name of author*) shall be the parliamentary authority of this club, subject to special rules which have been or will be adopted.

QUESTIONS

1.   What is the difference between the constitution and the by-laws of an organization?

2.   What essentials should be put in every constitution?

3.   What do the by-laws usually contain?

4.   In what form should a constitution and by-laws be written?

SUGGESTION FOR PRACTICE

1.   Write the constitution and by-laws for a dramatic club according to the model, observing the correct use of *articles*, *sections*, and forms of verbs (such as *shall be* or *may be*).

CHAPTER X

ORDER OF EXERCISES

A CERTAIN order of exercises in conducting a meeting is followed to give each item of business a proper place and to insure its consideration. This order is:

1. Call to order
   (Roll call)
2. Minutes
3. Reports of officers
4. Reports of committees
5. Unfinished business
6. New business
7. Program
8. Adjournment

The call to order is accomplished by the presiding officer striking the table with a gavel and saying, "The meeting will please come to order." If an accurate record of attendance is required, the secretary should call the roll at this time.

The minutes of the meeting or meetings of (insert dates) should then be read and approved. The presiding officer says, "We will listen to the reading of the minutes of the meeting of —— ——." The secretary stands, addresses the chair and members, and reads the minutes. The presiding officer then says, "Are there

56

any corrections to the minutes?" At this point corrections may be made by any member. If there is difference of opinion about a correction, it should be settled by vote of the club. No corrections being made, the presiding officer says, "If there are no corrections, the minutes stand approved as read. They are approved."

Reports of officers should be made at this time. The presiding officer may make known his ideas and plans to the club by reading a written report.

Any communications addressed to a club are next read by the secretary. Each should be disposed of by the proper motion before another is read.

The treasurer makes a report of receipts and disbursements. A motion to accept this report and place on file or enter in the minutes is then in order.

Reports of committees is the next order of business, and the presiding officer calls on each standing and special committee to report. Each report is disposed of as it is made.

Under *unfinished business* the presiding officer should bring up any motions postponed at a previous meeting, presenting these motions for discussion without asking for unfinished business.

Under the heading of *new business* any propositions not previously presented may be made in the form of motions and discussed by the members.

The program for the day follows.

Adjournment takes place after a motion to adjourn is made and carried; or, if all business is completed, the presiding officer may declare the meeting adjourned.

"Come to Order!"

QUESTIONS

1. How should a meeting be called to order?
2. How should corrections to the minutes be made?
3. When should communications to the club be read?
4. What action should be taken after each committee report?
5. What should be taken up under *unfinished business* ?
6. In what two ways may a meeting be adjourned?

SUGGESTION FOR PRACTICE

1. Suppose you are the president of a music club; write out the order of exercises which you might use in presiding at one of the meetings.

TEST

Fill in the blanks with correct word or words.

1. The chairman, —— the table with a ——, says: "The —— will please —— to ——. We will listen to the —— of the —— of the —— of January second."
2. "Are there any —— to the ——? If there are — ——, the —— stand —— as ——. We will listen to the —— of the treasurer."
3. "Is there a —— from the program ——?"
4. "What is your pleasure under new ——?"
5. "If there is no other business, we shall proceed with the —— for the day."
6. "If there is no further ——, the meeting is ——."

CHAPTER XI

OFFICERS AND MEMBERS

THE *presiding officer* may be called a speaker, a chairman, or a president, and is addressed as Mr. or Madam Speaker, Chairman, or President. He speaks of himself as *the chair* and should never say *I* when presiding. He may not make, second, or discuss a motion while occupying the chair. If he wishes to do so, he should call upon the vice-president to preside and should follow the regular rules applying to members. The presiding officer always has the right to vote, but he does not usually do so except when the vote is by ballot or roll call.

His duties are:

1. To be regular and prompt in attendance
2. To call meetings to order at the appointed time
3. To keep order
4. To recognize members
5. To state motions
6. To confine debate to the motion under discussion
7. To put motions to vote and announce the results
8. To decide points of order promptly

9. To stand when (a) stating a motion; (b) putting a motion to vote and declaring results; (c) speaking on questions of order.

The qualifications of a good presiding officer are a thorough understanding of parliamentary law and a tactful, impartial, and dignified manner at all times. The success of a meeting depends largely upon the skill and dispatch with which the chairman presides.

It is the duty of a *vice-president* to preside when the president is absent or when called to the chair by the president. Consequently he should be selected with great care. In case of a vacancy in the office of president, he must perform the duties of presiding officer until a new president is elected. Therefore he should acquaint himself with the duties and responsibilities of that office.

The duties of a *secretary* are:

1. To call the roll if required
2. To keep an accurate record of all proceedings
3. To keep the constitution and by-laws and all other papers belonging to the organization
4. To send out all notices required by the organization
5. To call the meeting to order in the absence of the president and vice-president and to preside while a temporary chairman is elected
6. To prepare for the chairman an order of business and a list of all committees

The way in which a secretary carries out these duties is extremely important to the success of an organization.

The secretary does not forfeit the right to make motions or to vote. In case of his absence a temporary secretary must be elected. In organizations where there is a great deal of correspondence, there may be a special secretary for that work.

The *treasurer* should keep an accurate record, written in ink, of all money received and paid out. The book containing this record should be owned by the society. He should insist on a receipt or voucher from every person or firm to whom he pays money.

He should never pay out money except on proper authority. The treasurer's book should be audited once or twice each year. His report should be written in the following form:

To the Parliamentary Law Club:

Your treasurer respectfully submits the following report of receipts and disbursements for the month of January, 1941:

<pre>
January 1
     Balance on hand $50.00

                    Receipts
January 15
     From E. L. S., Dues $ 5.00
               Total receipts $ 5.00
                                  ———— $55.00
</pre>

"Come to Order!"

Disbursements

January 21		
Paid J. C. Brown	$25.00	
January 30		
Paid A. L. Cook	$10.50	
Total disbursements		$35.50
January 31 Balance		$19.50
Total		$55.00

J. B. CUMMINGS, *Treasurer*

It is the duty of *every member* of a club to assist in maintaining a club spirit and to be loyal to the officers elected. A member should take the part assigned to him cheerfully and be familiar with parliamentary law. He should consider it his duty as well as his privilege to vote on all questions. He must not talk while another is talking nor pass between a presiding officer and any member who has the floor.

QUESTIONS

1. How should a presiding officer speak of himself?
2. May a chairman vote? Make motions?
3. When should a presiding officer stand?
4. Describe an ideal president.
5. Why should a vice-president be selected with great care?
6. What are the chief duties of a secretary?

7. What are the duties of a treasurer?

8. Study the form in which a treasurer's report is written. Write an original report.

9. What authority should a treasurer have before he pays out money?

10. What responsibility ought a good club member to take for the success of a meeting?

CHAPTER XII

ELECTION OF OFFICERS

CANDIDATES for office may be nominated from the floor by any member or by a nominating committee. If nominations are made by a committee, it is still permissible to nominate from the floor. Sometimes a nominating ballot is taken in order to find out the choices of the members. Nominations do not have to be seconded. A motion to close nominations may be made and, if carried by a two-thirds vote, stops further nominations.

The method of election may be provided for by the constitution or by the vote of the organization. The usual method is by ballot; but a rising vote, show of hands, or roll call may be taken. A motion that the secretary be instructed to cast a unanimous ballot for a certain officer may not be made, because this is contrary to the purpose of voting by ballot.

In balloting, one officer may be elected at a time, or the names of all the nominees may be put on one ballot and voted for at the same time. Ballots should be uniform. Tellers are usually appointed by the chairman to count the ballots. The methods of nomination and election, the kind of ballots, and any other preliminary arrangements should be decided upon before the day of electing officers.

In counting the ballots the tellers should discard all blank ballots as waste paper and count as illegal any ballots folded together and any cast for a person who is ineligible. Great care should be taken in counting the ballots; and a written report of all votes cast for each officer and the total number of votes should be read by the chairman of the tellers.

Tellers' Report

Number of votes cast	44
Illegal or void votes	6
Necessary for election.	20
Mr. Wright.	21
Mr. Chapman	17

A. J. PARKS,
CHARLES SMITH, *Tellers*

The ballots should be preserved as long as there is any probability of a request for a recount or until a motion is made to destroy them.

QUESTIONS

1. In what ways may candidates for office be nominated?
2. Do nominations have to be seconded?
3. How may nominations be closed?

4. How is the method to be used in electing officers provided for?

5. What preliminary arrangements should be made before an election?

6. What information should the tellers' report contain?

TEST

Are these statements about elections of officers true or false?

1. Officers must be elected by ballot.

2. A motion to close nominations requires a two-thirds vote.

3. The secretary may cast a unanimous ballot for an officer.

4. The duty of a teller is to nominate candidates.

5. There should be a written report of all votes cast.

6. Nominations must be seconded.

7. Candidates for office may be nominated from the floor.

8. The method of election may be provided for by the constitution.

9. Ballots used in an election should be destroyed as soon as they are counted.

10. The duty of a nominating committee is to give the result of an election.

CHAPTER XIII

ORGANIZATION PROCEDURE

WHENEVER a group of people wish to organize a society, this accepted method of procedure should be followed:

1. Call to order by any person
2. Election of a temporary chairman
3. Election of a temporary secretary
4. Statement of the object of the meeting
5. Adoption of a resolution that a society be formed
6. Appointment of a committee to draft a constitution and by-laws
7. Report of the committee
8. Adoption of the constitution
9. Adoption of the by-laws
10. Election of officers

An organization meeting may be arranged for by any persons interested in forming a society. When this meeting is held, anyone may rise, call the meeting to order, and say, "I nominate Mr. A. as chairman of this meeting. All those in favor say 'Aye.' All those opposed say 'No.'" If Mr. A. is elected, he takes the chair. If not, other nominations may be made and voted on. A secretary is next nominated and voted on

in the same manner. These officers serve until the permanent officers are elected.

When this temporary organization is completed, the
chairman calls upon some person especially interested
to state the object of the meeting. An informal discussion may follow, or a resolution may be offered at once
to form a society. For example, "I move the adoption
of the following resolution: *Resolved*, That this assembly organize itself into a Parliamentary Study
Club."

This motion is treated as any main motion. If the
resolution is adopted, the next order of business is a
motion that a committee be appointed to draft a constitution and by-laws. Sometimes a tentative constitution and by-laws are drawn up by those interested,
and proposed at this time, so that an organization may
be effected at the first meeting. If the framing of a
constitution and by-laws is left to a committee, a motion
to adjourn to meet at some definite time and place is in
order. This completes the usual business of the first
meeting.

At the second meeting the chairman calls the meeting
to order, and the minutes of the first meeting are read
and approved. The next order of business is the report
of the committee on the constitution and by-laws.
After this report is read, the chairman of the committee
or any person eligible to membership may move the
adoption of the constitution. Following the seconding

and stating of this motion, the chairman reads the constitution, section by section, allowing opportunity for discussion and amendment of each section as read. After this has been done, the chairman says, "The whole constitution is now open to amendment." When all desired amendments have been made, the main motion to adopt the constitution as amended is voted upon.

At this time all those who desire to become members may sign the constitution. A recess is usually taken so that this may be done before the next order of business. Only those who have signed the constitution, thus becoming members, may take part in the subsequent business.

The next order of business may be either the election of permanent officers or the adoption of the by-laws. The by-laws should be adopted in the same manner as the constitution. The adoption of the constitution and by-laws and the election of officers may all be done at the second meeting. If time does not permit, a third meeting may be held to complete the organization. The permanent officers take office as soon as elected. The newly elected president appoints the standing committees, specified by the by-laws, as soon as possible. This completes the organization of a society. If the time of the next meeting is not stated in the by-laws, a motion providing for the time should be made before adjournment.

"Come to Order!"

QUESTIONS

1. What are the three main steps in organizing a society?

2. Who may call an organization meeting? Who presides?

3. How is the object of this meeting presented to the assembly?

4. Who drafts the constitution and by-laws?

5. What is the method of procedure in adopting a constitution and by-laws?

6. How is the membership of the organization determined?

7. When do the permanent officers take office?

SUGGESTION FOR PRACTICE

1. Suppose you are interested in the organization of a garden club; write out the procedure for the first and second organization meetings and a possible third.

CHAPTER XIV

KINDS OF MEETINGS

Meetings of an organization are of three kinds: regular, special, and annual.

Regular meetings are provided for in the constitution or by-laws. At these meetings any business may be done which is in accordance with the purpose of the society and which the constitution allows. The order of exercises for regular meetings has been described in Chapter X.

Special meetings are called in the manner provided for in the constitution. The only business that may be done at a special meeting is that for which the meeting is called. The minutes of the previous regular meeting should not be read and approved unless notice was given of this in the call. The order of exercises is:

1. Call to order
2. Reading of call
3. Business included in the call in the order given

Annual meetings are different from regular meetings only in having a different order of exercises, which includes annual reports and election of officers.

"Come to Order!"

Officers should give reports of the year's work at this time. The order of exercises is:

1. Call to order
2. Reading of minutes
3. Annual reports of officers
4. Address of president
5. New business
6. Election of officers
7. Adjournment

If the business of any of these meetings cannot be completed for lack of time, an adjourned meeting may be held, which is a continuation of the first meeting. Any business in order at the first meeting is in order at the adjourned meeting.

QUESTIONS

1. Name three kinds of meetings that a society may hold.

2. What business may be done at a regular meeting?

3. Why are special meetings sometimes held? What business may be done at these meetings?

4. May the minutes of a regular meeting be read at a special meeting?

5. What is the order of exercises at a special meeting?

6. What special business is taken up at an annual meeting?

CHAPTER XV

PROCEDURE FOR A FORMAL DEBATE

In the conduct of a formal debate a presiding officer needs more than a knowledge of parliamentary law; he must be acquainted also with the procedure in this special type of meeting.

There is, however, no fixed set of rules for conducting a debate; interscholastic debating procedure is largely a matter of custom and agreement. There are, then, several different types of debate, the most common of which are the American plan and the British, or open-forum, plan. Since the American procedure is generally used in this country—though the open-forum plan is gaining in popularity—it is the American plan which will be described in detail here.

The officers of a debate under the American plan are the chairman, one or two time-keepers, and one or three judges. The chairman's position is the rear center of the stage or platform. He should be provided with a chair and a table. The time-keepers should sit together in the audience, directly in front of the platform. The judges may sit anywhere they desire in the audience, but they must not sit together.

All the members of both debating teams have positions on the platform, the affirmative team on the chair-man's right, and the negative on his left. For each team there should be provided chairs and a table. A pitcher of water and glasses on each table are generally welcome accessories. Still another table—a speaker's table—should be placed in the front center of the stage. Each speaker in turn may use this table for books and other reference material he may need while making his speech.

The chairman of the debate has several duties. He preserves order and does whatever else is necessary to insure courtesy and fair play. It is his duty to an-nounce the subject of the debate and the time allowed the speakers, to give instructions to the judges, to intro-duce each speaker in turn, and to announce the decision of the judges. He must be strictly impartial.

The time-keepers give each speaker two time-signals. The first is a one-minute warning before the time limit is reached. To give the signal one of the time-keepers rises and remains standing until the speaker recognizes him by nodding. When the time limit is reached, both time-keepers rise and remain standing until the speaker finishes. He is allowed only time enough to finish his sentence. The time-keepers may give signals by merely raising their hands instead of rising.

The duty of the judge or judges is to decide which side has won the debate. If there are three judges, each one shall give one vote, either affirmative or negative, without conferring with the others. At the close of the debate, each writes his decision on the ballot provided for him, signs it, seals it, and sends it by an usher to the chairman. If there is only one judge, he should be an expert, that is, one who knows the technicalities of debate as well as the subject debated. It is his duty not only to give his decision but also to explain it clearly and definitely to the audience. If possible, a critic-judge should give constructive criticisms of the speeches of each debater.

The order of procedure for a chairman to follow is:

1. Announcement of the proposition for debate.
2. Announcement of sides.
3. Announcement of the time for the constructive speeches and the rebuttal speeches.
4. Announcement of judges and instructions to them.
5. Reading of the interpretation of the question.
6. Introduction of the speakers for their constructive speeches.
7. Introduction of the speakers for their rebuttal speeches.
8. Repetition of instructions to judges.
9. Announcement of decision of judges.

In opening a debate, the chairman usually gives a few words of welcome first. He then reads the proposi-

tion and announces the sides to be taken by each team
and the names of the speakers representing each.
Next, he announces the time allowed for the constructive and rebuttal speeches. The chairman reads the
names of the judges, and for the benefit of both
the judges and the audience, he gives specific instructions on the points to be considered in judging the
debate.

Sometimes the chairman reads the interpretation of
the question as it is to be debated. More frequently
this interpretation is given by the first speaker of the
affirmative.

After this introduction, the chairman formally opens
the debate by saying, "Mr. Wilson will open the case
for the affirmative." At the conclusion of the first
speech, the negative side is introduced by the chairman,
who says, "Mr. Roger will open the case for the negative." The other affirmative and negative speakers
follow alternately. They are introduced by the chairman's saying, "Mr. Griffin will take up the case and
continue for the affirmative (or negative)."

Immediately following these constructive speeches,
the chairman introduces the speakers for the rebuttal.
The negative side opens the rebuttal. The chairman
introduces the first speaker by saying, "There will be a
five-minute rebuttal speech for the negative given by
Mr. Roger." Then the affirmative and negative sides
are introduced alternately. The debate is always closed

by the affirmative. The chairman introduces the final speaker by saying, "The debate will be closed by Mr. Wilson of the affirmative."

Immediately following the debate, it is well for the chairman to repeat the instructions given to the judges, thus reminding them and the audience of the points upon which the debate is to be judged.

When the chairman has received the ballots of the judges, he opens the sealed envelopes in the presence of the audience and announces the decision. As a matter of courtesy, the number of votes on each side is not given. If there is a critic-judge, the chairman calls him to the platform and introduces him to the audience to give his decision and criticisms.

The chairman must not allow himself to be confused as to what constitutes a question of order. Occasionally, an interscholastic debater on the negative side rises to a point of order during the closing speech made by the affirmative. The attempt is thus made by the negative side to impress the judges and audience with the idea that the negative case has been misquoted or misunderstood by the affirmative. A question of parliamentary procedure, however, is not involved and the chairman of the debate should not allow the mistake to be made. A question of order may be raised in a debate only when some supposed mistake in debating procedure is made, such, for example, as speaking out of turn.

"Come to Order!"

In the British, or open-forum system of debating, each side of the proposition is presented by one or more speakers. It is the duty of the chairman to introduce these speakers to the audience. Then follows an open-forum with several speakers from the floor. When the question is opened to the audience for discussion, the chairman should insist that the rules of parliamentary law governing the discussion of a motion be observed by all. The decision in this type of debating is made by the audience. This may be done by a division of the house. If a more formal vote is desired, ballots may be used. These may be collected and counted while the open-forum is still in progress.

There are several innovations in the forms of debating. One of these, the "Oregon Plan," follows the form of court procedure. In this plan, the chairman acts as judge, and has power to rule concerning the relevancy of material, to demand definition, and to limit discussion to a point.

QUESTIONS

1. What types of debates are commonly used?
2. What stage or platform arrangements should be made for a debate?
3. Name the duties of a chairman.
4. How are time signals given?
5. How should the judges give their decision? A critic-judge?

6. What is the order of procedure for conducting a debate according to the American plan?
7. How should the speakers be introduced?
8. In what order should the rebuttal speeches be given?
9. How should the chairman announce the decision of the judges?
10. What is the procedure in a debate conducted according to the British plan?

REVIEW TEST

Which are true and which are false statements?

1. The first order of business in an organization meeting is to elect permanent officers.
2. A temporary chairman presides at an organization meeting.
3. A constitution is drafted by those present at an organization meeting.
4. The by-laws are part of the constitution.
5. Permanent officers take office as soon as elected.
6. A constitution describes the government of an organization.
7. It should be easy to amend a constitution.
8. The by-laws contain rules governing the action of club members.
9. Candidates for office must be nominated by ballot.
10. It is the duty of tellers to count the ballots.

11. A presiding officer has the right to vote.

12. A chairman may discuss a motion while he is presiding.

13. A presiding officer should speak of himself as the chair.

14. A chairman should state all motions made by members.

15. A chairman should always announce the result of a vote on a motion.

16. A secretary does not have the right to vote.

17. A secretary should have his books audited every year.

18. It is not necessary for the members of an organization to understand parliamentary law if the president does.

19. A member must vote on all motions.

20. A chairman should follow a certain order of exercises in conducting a meeting.

21. Unfinished business is the first order of business in a meeting.

22. The minutes of a meeting must be approved by the members of an organization.

23. The report on a question which has been referred to a committee at a previous meeting is made under the heading of new business.

24. The purpose of a committee of the whole is to give club members an opportunity for informal discussion on some subject.

25. All committee reports should be in writing.

26. Standing committees must be elected and special committees appointed.

27. Minutes should contain a brief account of the discussion on each motion.

28. Any business may be brought up at a special meeting.

29. There is a special order of exercises for an annual meeting.

30. An adjourned meeting may only be held to finish the business of a regular meeting.

31. The chairman presiding over a debate instructs the judges how to vote.

32. The American system of interscholastic debating allows each member of both teams to speak twice.

PART II. GROUP DISCUSSION

INTRODUCTION

Young people today, as well as people in general, find themselves face to face with problems of increasing complexity.   In school and college the student is asking what he can expect in the world of work.   He is puzzled when he contemplates taking his part as a citizen on election day.   He wonders how he can make up his mind about any of the great national or international problems.   Citizens everywhere feel baffled by these same questions.   How can one person alone find answers to such complex problems?   No one individual has all the facts at hand.   Moreover, he lacks the time to search for these facts, and the sources from which to collect them.   Without them it is difficult to form sound judgments.

It is reasonable, therefore, to suppose that he can find help by talking over these problems with other people in discussion groups.   Here he can pool his knowledge and share his ideas and experiences with others under the guidance of a leader.   In this way he can increase his own knowledge, and the group, thinking co-operatively, may create new ways of solving problems.   Such creative thinking, undertaken by all, frequently brings about a better solution than that which any one person could have thought out alone.

Group discussion is not a contest between opposing sides. Rather, it is an effort to work together toward a common conclusion. "Group discussion is not an argument nor a debate," according to Harrison S. Elliott in *The Process of Group Thinking*. "In an argument the persons representing each side usually have their minds made up. Their purpose is to convince or defeat their opponents. In genuine discussion, on the other hand, folk come with open mind and with problems, expecting to get new light on their problems in working with others in search for a solution." [1]

In true discussion, then, a group is trying to think reflectively. To do this requires an understanding of the process of reflective thinking as described by Professor Dewey in *How We Think*. The steps in this process, simplified, are:

1. See the difficulty
2. State and define the problem
3. Sift the facts and explore solutions
4. Seek help from added facts
5. Select a solution and test it [2]

Group discussion that satisfies does not just happen. It must be learned by all who are to take part in it successfully. It can be best learned by *doing* it, under a

[1] Reprinted by permission of Association Press.
[2] Reprinted by permission of D. C. Heath and Company.

leader who is experienced in guiding people through the steps of reflective thinking. The role played by a good leader is explained in Chapter XVI.

Informal group discussion is best suited to a small group of ten or twelve people. However, a large learning group also may benefit from group discussion, but it must use special devices. Two important devices are (1) the panel, and (2) the steering committee. These may be used in a class of forty, in a club meeting of a hundred people, or in a conference of several hundred. The panel will be explained in Chapter XVII; the steering committee, in Chapter XVIII.

Group discussion is a valuable tool in problem-solving both in the school and in life outside the school. In school it may be used in the classroom, in clubs, in student associations, and, particularly, in the core curriculum groups. Teaching the use of this tool may well be a part of the school curriculum. Outside the school it is of great value in many organizations, such as churches and literary and civic clubs—in fact, wherever people are trying to understand and to solve the problems that arise.

QUESTIONS

1. What results may be expected from group discussion?

2. What is the difference between argument and group discussion?

3. What are the five steps in reflective thinking?

4. What is the best way to learn how to take part in group discussion?

5. How large a group is best suited for informal discussion?

6. By what devices may large learning groups enjoy the advantages of small-group discussion?

EXERCISES

1. Test your ability to explain clearly the meaning of each of the following terms:

> Group discussion
> Argument
> Debate
> Reflective thinking
> Creative thinking

2. Give an example illustrating each type of problem mentioned in the first paragraph of this chapter.

> a. Why is it difficult for one person alone to find the answers to these problems?
> b. Show how group discussion can aid in solving these problems.

CHAPTER XVI

HOW TO LEAD A GROUP DISCUSSION

To BE an effective leader of a group discussion requires a quality of leadership different from that expected of a club president or a chairman presiding over a formal debate. The role of a group-discussion leader is to stimulate the members of a group to think, and to guide them through the steps of reflective thinking. In general, he leads the members of a group as they work together to find answers to the following questions:

1. What is the situation here?
   a. What are the difficulties?
   b. What people or things are affected by it?
   c. What is the common interest that unites the members of the group?
2. What can be done about the problem?
   a. What are the possible solutions?
   b. What are the probable outcomes of each solution?
   c. What are the facts and opinions on which the members of the group agree?
   d. What are the facts and opinions on which they differ?
   e. What added facts or opinions can be secured?

f. What solution of the problem seems best for all concerned?

3. How can it be done?

   What are the ways and means for carrying out the decision reached?

In searching for the answers to these questions the members of the group are following the steps in reflective thinking.

ACTIVITIES

1. A high school graduating class wishes to make a gift to the school. You are the class president. Prepare a list of questions based on those above for the class to consider.

2. Suppose your speech class is studying group discussion. Divide the class into groups of ten or twelve. Have each group select a topic on some school problem and conduct a discussion on it.

   a. Choose a leader.
   b. Arrange the seating so that the group may sit face-to-face, if possible.
   c. Practice group discussion, following the five steps in reflective thinking.
   d. Ask the teacher and the listening groups to appraise each discussion.

Did each leader use the questions suggested above to guide the group in the discussion?

Did each group follow the process of reflective thinking according to the five steps given in the introduction?

How to Lead a Group Discussion

The person selected to lead a discussion must have special personal qualifications. First, he should have an open-minded attitude; that is, he must be impartial and unbiased, and make sure that all points of view are presented. Second, he should have the ability to reason, and should be a ready speaker who can be easily heard. Third, he should possess a sense of humor; this will help him greatly in maintaining a friendly atmosphere in the group and may save many a tense situation. Most of all, he must have patience and must keep in mind that thinking a problem through to a solution is a slow process both for the individual and for the whole group.

Even though a chairman is selected for his wide knowledge and understanding of the problem to be discussed and for his skill in leading a discussion, he still must make careful preparation. His preparation should include:

1. Making an outline
2. Foreseeing the probable course of the discussion
3. Becoming acquainted with the members of the discussion group
4. Checking the physical setting

The outline should include a carefully thought out definition of the problem to be discussed, a list of the important issues involved, possible solutions, his own tentative conclusion, and ways of putting his solution into operation.

"Come to Order!"

Select one of the following problems and prepare a leader's outline to use in conducting a discussion.

a. What is the best grading system for a high school?
b. Should athletes in college receive free tuition?
c. Should motion pictures be censored?

The leader should try to foresee the probable course of the discussion and plan what he could do in this or that case if unusual circumstances should develop.

The leader should make every effort possible to become acquainted with the members of the group before the meeting so that he may better understand their points of view and their attitudes toward the question under discussion. He will be better able to keep harmony if he knows in advance who may need to be brought back to the topic, who may need to be calmed down tactfully, and who may need to be stimulated to express his ideas.

He should consult with the general arrangements committee, if he is not a member of it, to be sure that a suitable physical setting is being arranged and that everything will be in readiness for the meeting to begin on time.

One discussion technique which the leader frequently overlooks is that of creating a friendly atmosphere in which to start. A few well-chosen words of welcome which will bring out the common interest of the group and the reason for their meeting at this particular time will do much toward starting the discussion in the right direction and with the proper spirit.

ACTIVITY

Imagine your class as a small discussion group. Choose a problem for discussion and write an introduction for a leader to give in starting the discussion.

After the leader has stated the problem and the discussion is under way, he must be alert to prevent its wandering aimlessly and thus arriving nowhere. This does not mean that he should arbitrarily direct the discussion—rather, he should allow it to proceed freely along democratic lines. But it is his responsibility to keep the discussion to the point.

SOME HELPFUL SUGGESTIONS TO THE LEADER FOR GUIDING DISCUSSION

1. *Aid the non-aggressive member to express his point of view.* You can do this by watching his facial expression and encouraging him by a smile to enter the discussion, or by asking him what he thinks about the question under discussion.

2. *Guard against needless repetition.* When all the ideas on one point seem to have been expressed, you should see to it that the discussion is advanced to the consideration of some further point.

3. *See that all phases of the topic are treated.* You should know from your outline, prepared in advance, whether a certain phase of the topic has been neglected. If you know that someone in the group is able to bring out a point that has been overlooked, you should ask him to do so. Otherwise, you yourself may quote the opinion of someone outside the group, and then ask for a discussion of it.

4. *Announce the progress of the discussion.* Just as a radio announcer tells his audience the progress of a base-ball game after each inning, so you, as the leader of a discussion, should, from time to time, announce what-ever points of agreement have been reached, and what points are still open for discussion because of lack of agreement. This will help to keep the group aware of the progress they are making.

5. *Summarize the discussion.* Just as the radio announcer of a baseball game gives, after the game is over, a summary of the important and decisive plays in order that the whole game may be understood, so you should give a final account of the points raised, of the agreements reached, and any differences not harmo-nized, so that the entire pattern may be clear.

Some Suggestions for Dealing with Members Who Hinder the Progress of a Discussion

1. To the *member who wanders from the subject* the leader may say: "The ideas that you are presenting are

interesting, but they do not seem to apply to the subject under discussion, do they? Perhaps we can discuss them at another time."

2. To the *member who talks too long* the leader may say: "We are sorry that the time for this discussion is limited. Your point is so and so. We thank you for your contribution. May we hear from other members now?"

3. To the *member who talks too often* the leader may say: "Since we have not heard from everyone yet, would you mind postponing what you were about to say until after the others have spoken?"

4. To the *member who interrupts* the leader should say, in a dignified manner, that the parliamentary rule with respect to one person's having the floor at a time applies to an informal discussion. But the leader should be quick to distinguish between the member who merely interrupts and one who calls attention to an emergency. The latter should, of course, be heard.

5. To the *member who makes angry or sarcastic remarks* the leader, in a dignified manner, should say that the group is searching for truth, and that the discussion must not become a battle-ground because of personal antagonism. Sound reasoning and a co-operative spirit must prevail throughout the discussion.

6. To the *member who asks irrelevant questions* the leader should tactfully explain why such a question may not be answered at this time.

"Come to Order!"

Some Warnings to the Leader

1. *Don't dominate the discussion.* Your role is to stimulate and lead group-thinking.

2. *Don't comment on each contribution as it is made.* You will impede the progress of the discussion by so doing.

3. *Don't answer questions yourself.* Your part is to draw out answers from the group.

4. *Don't summarize too often.* Your summary should only mark each step in the discussion.

5. *Don't rush the discussion.* Try to set a pace that the average member of the group is able to maintain.

6. *Don't express an opinion.* You should remain impartial.

7. *Don't allow the meeting to drag or to overrun the time set.* You should close the meeting on time.

QUESTIONS

1. What is the role of a leader in group discussion?

2. What personal qualifications should a leader of group discussions have?

3. What preparation should a leader of group discussion make?

4. How can a leader encourage the timid member to take part in a discussion?

5. How can a leader bring out points that have been neglected in a discussion?

6. When should a leader summarize the progress made in a discussion?

7. How should a leader summarize a discussion?

8. How can a leader keep the members on the subject they are discussing?

9. How can a leader deal with a member who monopolizes the discussion?

10. How can a leader prevent a discussion from becoming an argument?

EXERCISES

1. The pupils in a core curriculum group have selected group discussion as a tool which they need to know how to use. Let several members of the group take turns in planning a discussion and in leading one under the guidance of the teacher. Ask the teacher and the other members of the group to write constructive criticisms of the way in which the discussion was led, and also to judge whether or not the steps in reflective thinking were followed.

2. Let several members of the class attend a meeting of some discussion group in the community, and then report to the class upon the effectiveness of the leader. The report should supply answers to the following questions:

    a. Did the leader seem to be well chosen for his personal qualifications?

    b. Did he seem to be well prepared for leading the discussion?

    c. Did he create a friendly atmosphere in which to start?

    d. Did he state the problem clearly?

e. Did he aid the non-aggressive member to take part in the discussion?

f. Did he take care that all points of view should be brought out?

g. Did he handle any difficult situation tactfully?

h. Did he guide the discussion through the steps of reflective thinking?

i. Did he summarize well?

j. Did he close the meeting on time?

CHAPTER XVII

THE PANEL

THE *panel* is one of the best modern devices for securing for large learning groups the advantages of small group discussion. In this type of discussion a small group carries on an informal conversation upon some problem in front of a larger group. After listening to this conversation, the members of the larger group may contribute their own ideas to the discussion or may ask questions. During the entire discussion all should be trying to understand one another's points of view. The result aimed at in a panel discussion is not usually the solution of a problem; rather, it is the clearer understanding of all sides of a problem that comes to a person from listening to a thoughtful conversation about it. This understanding will give him a basis upon which to make his own decision.

In a panel discussion there are three distinct factors:
1. The chairman
2. The panel
3. The audience

The *chairman* sets the tone of the whole meeting. Too much importance cannot be placed upon his selection. He must have a general understanding of the problem that is to be discussed, and he must be skillful in the technique of leading a discussion.

The *panel* is made up of from four to eight persons. Each member of the panel should be selected because he represents a definite point of view on the problem under discussion or because he is an expert in the field. As an individual, he should be open-minded, and should be able to think creatively and to speak clearly. The panel discussion will prove most satisfactory if the members chosen are of nearly equal ability and prestige.

The *audience* is the third factor. It is taken for granted that the audience is present to gain something and then to give something. Its part, therefore, is to listen carefully to the discussion of the panel members and to participate in turn.

It is important to have the proper atmosphere for a panel discussion. A committee on arrangements may create this atmosphere by selecting a suitable room for the meeting and by planning the stage setting. The room should be quiet, well lighted and ventilated, and large enough to seat everyone comfortably. The stage setting should be one that makes informal conversation easy. The members of the panel should be seated in comfortable chairs at an oval table facing the audience, or at smaller tables arranged so as to preserve the semi-circle. The chairman should be seated in the center, definitely a part of the panel. By this arrangement, all

The Panel

the members of the panel can see one another, and all can be seen by the audience.

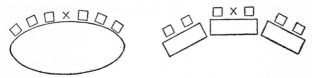

1. Plan the best possible arrangement of your classroom for holding a panel discussion.

2. Make a survey of your school building and select the room that is best adapted for creating the proper atmosphere for a panel discussion.

3. Your school is trying to decide whether to adopt the plan of having a student-ticket of admission to all athletic activities. Plan a panel discussion on this problem to be held at a student assembly. Select a panel of students from various student groups, such as the student association, school clubs, the school paper, etc.; in this selection make sure that all student points of view will be represented. Justify your plan and your selection of the panel.

Preparation for a panel discussion should be made by each individual member of the panel. The more reading, assembling of facts, and reflective thinking each individual member can do in advance, the better able he will be to make worth-while contributions to the discussion. A preliminary meeting of the panel should be held to provide the members with an opportunity to become acquainted with one another, to talk over the rules, and to receive instructions from the chairman as to the procedure. However, there should be no actual rehearsal.

At the hour set for the discussion, the chairman rises and explains the rules to the audience:

1. He states how much time has been allotted for the panel discussion, and how much for the audience participation; for example, one hour for the panel, and one-half hour for the audience.

2. He explains that there are to be no set speeches, and that the rules of parliamentary procedure for obtaining the floor and for discussion need not be observed by the panel; but that the general rules of courtesy governing conversation are to be observed.

3. He suggests that it would be better to present one thought at a time.

4. He states that questions may be asked whenever they seem necessary to the reaching of a better understanding, but that there should be no arguing as in a formal debate; above all, that there should be no personal criticisms.

5. He explains that the purpose of a panel discussion is to clarify thought and to bring

about understanding, rather than to reach a decision.

Next, the chairman introduces each member of the panel.

The chairman then states the problem. He may define terms and set limits within which the discussion is to be kept. He also describes the situation as it appears to the members of the panel.

After this introduction, the chairman sits down and the conversation begins. The start may be made by some member voluntarily giving his point of view on the subject announced for discussion, or the chairman himself may start the ball rolling by asking some member to express his ideas on the topic. Occasionally it may seem best to ask each member of the panel to state his particular point of view in a two-minute speech before the informal conversation begins. While talking with one another, the panel members should constantly keep in mind that the discussion is being carried on for the benefit of the larger group.

The conversation continues until important factors influencing the problem have been brought out and are understood by all. From time to time the chairman summarizes important points of view and re-states the problem. The discussion then continues until the problem is fully analyzed, and the points of difference appear. The points of agreement are then summarized by the chairman, and the attention of the panel is

SUGGESTIONS FOR UNDERSTANDING ANOTHER PERSON'S POINT OF VIEW [1]

Best Techniques	Don'ts
Ask the other person what his point of view is	Don't reveal your own point of view
Compare the points of agreement and the points of conflict	Don't defend
Be curious	Don't be biased
Be an observer	Don't be resentful of the egotist
Ask questions	Don't say
I don't quite understand what you mean, did you say ——?	It seems to me
Will you re-state ——?	I still think
What do you think about (ignored facts) ——?	I believe
	I don't agree

Master Test for Understanding: "When you can state another person's point of view so perfectly that the other person unqualifiedly accepts your statement."

[1] This chart is an adaptation of techniques found in *Teachers and Cooperation*, by S. A. Courtis, E. T. McSwain, and Nellie C. Morrison. Reprinted by permission.

turned to the points of real difference. When there are no new points of view expressed and when the points of agreement and the points of real difference have been clearly brought out, the entire pattern as it appears to the panel may be seen.

Now the chairman will open the discussion to the audience. Anyone may contribute a point of view not brought out by the panel or ask questions for a better understanding of any ideas previously presented by the panel. During the discussion by the audience, parliamentary rules governing such matters as obtaining the floor and addressing all remarks to the chairman should be observed.

After the time allowed for audience questions and contributions has elapsed, the chairman closes the panel discussion with a final summary which brings together all the points of view that have been presented.

In selecting topics for panel discussions, the interests, experiences, abilities, and purposes of a group should be kept in mind. Only a topic about which members of the group are puzzled or uncertain, or on which there seems to be a difference of opinion, makes a good one for a panel discussion. It is best phrased in a complete sentence in the form of a question.

SUGGESTED TOPICS FOR PANEL DISCUSSION

1. Should the public schools offer two years of vocational training beyond high school?

"Come to Order!"

2. Is all propaganda harmful?
3. Should we establish state medicine?
4. Should the nations of the Western Hemisphere form a League of Nations?
5. Should organized lobbying be prohibited?
6. Is a free press endangered in America?
7. Can government service be made a career?
8. Should students in high school buy their own textbooks?
9. Should college football be subsidized?
10. Is America a good neighbor?
11. Should high-school fraternities and sororities be prohibited by state law?
12. Should the compulsory age limit for attending school be raised from sixteen to eighteen?

EXERCISE

Study the chart on page 102, and then practice trying to understand another person's point of view. Have a student state his opinion about the grading system used in his school. Let the members of the class ask him questions until his position is so clear to them that someone in the class can re-state his position so perfectly that he will unqualifiedly accept the statement.

QUESTIONS

1. What is a panel discussion?
2. What is the purpose of a panel discussion?
3. What result may be expected from a panel discussion?

The Panel

4. List the qualities that are desirable for the members of a panel.

5. What preparation should individual members of a panel make?

6. Why should a preliminary meeting of a panel be held?

7. List the usual rules followed in panel discussions.

8. What part is taken by the audience?

Activities

1. Social studies classes today are studying current national and international problems. Many of them subscribe to some current-event periodical. Plan a panel discussion on some problem presented in a periodical. Choose a leader for the discussion. Select five members of the class for the panel. Let the class be the audience. Have each member of the class prepare for his part in the discussion. After the discussion, have the class criticize the planning, the effectiveness of the leader, the panel, and the audience participation.

2. The forum-lecture is a widely used method of discussion in which one person makes a speech and then answers questions from the audience. Compare this with the panel method of discussion. Which do you consider more helpful in problem-solving? Why?

3. Besides the panel and the forum-lecture methods of discussion, there are the round table and the sym-

posium. The round table is a name applied to discussion groups in which all participate on an equal basis.
The symposium is a form of discussion in which, after
several persons have presented various phases of a
problem in separate speeches, there follows a ques-
tion-and-answer period. Such a discussion is presided
over by a chairman. People, generally, use the word
"forum" to name all these methods of discussion.

    a. Listen to radio discussion programs, such as
America's Town Meeting of the Air and the
University of Chicago Round Table. Compare these with the panel method of discussion. Do the speakers participating in these
programs defend their own ideas, or do they
try to understand one another's point of
view?

    b. Follow your daily newspaper for two weeks
for programs featuring group discussions.
List and classify these. Notice the type of
organization in which they are used. If
possible, attend one of these meetings, and
make a report to the class.

CHAPTER XVIII

STEERING COMMITTEES

IF IT is desired to combine the advantages of small-group discussion with large-group deliberation, a very useful device is the *steering committee*. A panel, as we have seen, is a device for carrying on informal group discussion in a large meeting itself. A steering committee, on the other hand, organizes the large learning group on a "group-thinking" basis by alternating meetings of small discussion groups with meetings of the large group. Thus an opportunity for democratic participation by all is provided.

The first step is to name a general chairman of the whole large group. Next, the large group is divided into several small discussion groups of about ten or twelve members each. Each discussion group should be made up of a cross-section of the entire group. A co-ordinator to lead the group and a recorder to keep a record of the discussion are chosen for each group. The co-ordinators and the general chairman of the large group together with one or two others, if so desired, act as a steering committee.

The procedure used by a steering committee is as follows:

"Come to Order!"

1. The steering committee meets to talk over the general problems of the large group and to suggest several of the most important ones for discussion.

2. The large group meets to decide on which problems to discuss.

3. The small groups meet to discuss these problems. The discussion held in each group is summarized by its recorder and a report is made to the steering committee by its co-ordinator.

4. The steering committee next consolidates these reports.

5. The large group meets again to hear the consolidated reports, to carry on further discussion, and to suggest possible solutions.

6. The small groups meet a second time to discuss fully the suggested solutions, and possibly to propose others.

7. The steering committee, in turn, consolidates all the suggested solutions and prepares a report for the large group.

8. The large group has its final meeting, to hear and to discuss the report of the steering committee and officially to adopt for action, if it so desires, the conclusions of the entire assembly worked out through the co-operative thinking of all.

Steering Committees

The effectiveness of the plan just outlined depends on the organizing ability of the steering committee and especially on the quality of co-operative thinking done in the meetings of the small discussion groups. The co-ordinators chosen to lead these groups should be skilled in guiding the group in reflective thinking.

This general plan may be adapted to meet the needs of almost any large learning group. It is frequently used today in the more progressive institutes and conferences.

So that we may see more clearly just how the democratic process of group-thinking may be carried on by means of this procedure, let us follow the work of a steering committee as it directs a conference on pupil needs, set up by a student association in a high school.

The chart on page 110 shows the organization of the steering committee for carrying on this conference and the division of the student body into small groups for discussion.

How the Conference Is Conducted

1. The steering committee meets to study problems of high school students and lists the following problems:

a. Safety	e. Manners and courtesy
b. Vocations	f. Preparation for college
c. Mental hygiene	g. Civic interests
d. Study habits	h. Student government

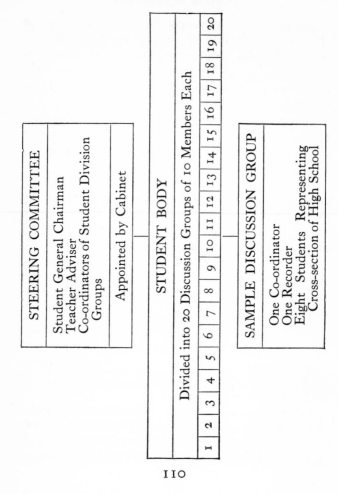

STEERING COMMITTEE

Student General Chairman
Teacher Adviser
Co-ordinators of Student Division Groups

Appointed by Cabinet

STUDENT BODY

Divided into 20 Discussion Groups of 10 Members Each

1	2	3	4	5	6	7	8	9	10	11	12	13	14	15	16	17	18	19	20

SAMPLE DISCUSSION GROUP

One Co-ordinator
One Recorder
Eight Students Representing Cross-section of High School

Steering Committees

2. The student body meets as a whole to hear the report of the steering committee and selects "Vocations" for discussion in the conference as the problem of greatest interest to the majority.

3. The small groups then meet to discuss their vocational needs. A summary of each discussion is made by the recorder of each group and is carried back to the steering committee by the co-ordinator.

4. The steering committee consolidates all the reports and finds that the twenty groups are in agreement, and that the important problems connected with the choice of a vocation are stated in the following questions:

  a. What jobs and careers are there today?
  b. What opportunities for jobs and careers are there in our community?
  c. What job or career am I best suited for?
  d. How can I find out about different jobs and careers?
  e. How can I fit myself for my job or my career?
  f. How can I find my job or my career?

5. The student body meets again to hear the report of the steering committee, to carry on further discussion, and to suggest possible answers.

6. The small groups meet a second time to discuss fully the proposed answers to their questions.

7. The steering committee then consolidates all the answers proposed by the separate groups and brought

back by the co-ordinators. It finds the results of the group-thinking to be a demand for the following:

a. A section of the high school library devoted to jobs and careers
b. A community survey of jobs and careers
c. Vocational guidance
d. Jobs and Careers Institute
e. More vocational education
f. A Placement Bureau

8. The student body has a final meeting to hear the report of the steering committee. After a discussion of the report, a motion is carried to request the Cabinet of the Student Association to draw up a set of resolutions covering the results of the group-thinking of this conference, to be presented to the high school faculty and the Board of Education.

It will be seen that the steering-committee device or procedure provides a method of discussion whereby a large group can work as a pure democracy. By it each member of the group is given an opportunity to take a personal part in co-operative thinking and planning; he does not have to leave the solution of problems that concern the whole group to representatives or committees which might propose only one solution which would be adopted through pressure or by the inertia of the group.

Steering Committees

QUESTIONS

1. Compare the steering committee and the panel as devices for giving large groups the advantages of informal group discussion.
2. Describe the plan used by a steering committee in carrying out its purpose.
3. How is the steering committee made up?
4. In the procedure carried out by a steering committee
   a. What are the various functions of the steering committee?
   b. What is the role of the small group?
   c. What work is done by the large group?
5. Upon what two things does the effectiveness of the plan used by a steering committee depend?

ACTIVITIES

1. Organize your class into a student conference. Choose a problem for discussion. Divide the class into small discussion groups. Provide for meetings of the small groups alternating with meeting of the entire group. Follow through the procedure for a conference as described in this chapter. Criticize and evaluate the way in which your class carried out this plan.
2. Make a survey of your school and find out where this plan for a conference could be used. Could it be used in (a) your student association? (b) your social studies class? (c) your athletic association? Work out a model plan for holding a conference in your school.

3. Study as many programs of institutes and conferences as you can find. What types of discussion
groups are used? Do you find any programs where
small group meetings alternate with meetings of the
entire conference?

INDEX

Index

Index

Index

Index

Index

Index

THINGS TO BE REMEMBERED—FOR MEMBERS

BEST FORMS AND PRACTICES	DON'T SAY
1. "I move that . . ." *or* "I move to . . ."	1. "I move you, Mr. Chairman," *or* "I make a motion."
2. "I second the motion."	2. "I support the motion."
3. Give opinion on the question after motion is stated by the chair.	3. "I move that . . . (and give reasons for motion)."
4. All debate should be confined to the motion under discussion.	4. Anything that does not relate to the motion under discussion.
5. Move the previous question to close debate and bring a question to vote.	5. "Question."
6. "I move to amend by inserting . . . , etc."	6. "I move to amend the motion so as to read . . ."
7. "I move to lay the question on the table."	7. "I move to lay the amendment on the table."